CONSERVATION CHAMPIONS!

CLEANING UP YOUR COMMUNITY

SADIE SILVA

Enslow PUBLISHING

Please visit our website, www.enslow.com.
For a free color catalog of all our high-quality books, call toll free 1-800-398-2504 or fax 1-877-980-4454.

Library of Congress Cataloging-in-Publication Data
Names: Silva, Sadie author
Title: Cleaning up your community / Sadie Silva.
Description: Buffalo, NY : Enslow Publishing, [2027] | Series: Conservation champions! | Includes index.
Identifiers: LCCN 2025055126 (print) | LCCN 2025055127 (ebook) | ISBN 9781978547650 library binding | ISBN 9781978547643 paperback | ISBN 9781978547667 ebook
Subjects: LCSH: Environmentalism | Refuse and refuse disposal | Volunteer workers in environmental protection | Volunteer workers in community development
Classification: LCC GE195.5 .S558 2027 (print) | LCC GE195.5 (ebook) | DDC 333.72–dc23/eng/20260309
LC record available at https://lccn.loc.gov/2025055126
LC ebook record available at https://lccn.loc.gov/2025055127

Published in 2027 by
Enslow Publishing
2544 Clinton Street
Buffalo, NY 14224

Designer: Tanya Dellaccio Keeney
Editor: Therese Shea

Photo credits: Cover (boy) Amorn Suriyan/Shutterstock.com; cover (garbage) Ichsan Gallery/Shutterstock.com; p. 5 Sergey Demo SVDPhoto/Shutterstock.com; p. 7 (squirrel) Photography by Gretchen/Shutterstock.com; p. 7 (deer) Cristi Croitoru/Shutterstock.com; p. 9 David W. Leindecker/Shutterstock.com; p. 11 mingis/Shutterstock.com; p. 13 (man) Michaelpuche/Shutterstock.com; p. 13 (sign) Dalton Sipe/Shutterstock.com; p. 15 Rawpixel.com/Shutterstock.com; p. 17 (sign) Steve Skjold/Shutterstock.com; pp. 17 (people), 19 Zamrznuti tonovi/Shutterstock.com; p. 21 Studio Romantic/Shutterstock.com.

Printed in the United States of America

CPSIA compliance information: Batch #CSENS27: For further information contact Enslow Publishing, at 1-800-398-2504.

CONTENTS

BOLDFACE WORDS APPEAR IN THE GLOSSARY.

GROSS GARBAGE

Have you ever taken a walk and come across garbage, or trash, on the ground? That can ruin a nice time. It isn't just ugly to look at. It's bad for many reasons. That's why it's important for people to work together to clean up their communities.

GARBAGE BELONGS IN A TRASH CAN, NOT IN NATURE.

TERRIBLE TRASH

Trash that isn't thrown away correctly is called litter. It can be dangerous to animals. Animals may get trapped in it. It might look like food or smell like food to them. They may try to eat it. Some litter can make them sick or even kill them.

PLASTIC BAGS CAN BE VERY DANGEROUS TO ANIMALS.

MORE POLLUTION PROBLEMS

Some kinds of **pollution** are less easy to see. You may not be able to see **chemicals** dumped in dirt or in waterways. Buried garbage can break down into smaller pieces of harmful matter. These things are still dangerous to animals and plants.

WIND AND WATER CAN CARRY LITTER AWAY FROM WHERE IT WAS DROPPED.

Pollution doesn't just ruin nature for plants and animals. It can ruin nature for people. Polluted water is unhealthy for people to swim in, for example. Broken glass in parks and on playgrounds is dangerous for children too.

GOVERNMENTS TRY TO KEEP PEOPLE SAFE, BUT NOT ALL POLLUTION CAN BE SEEN.

BEACH
CLOSED
POLLUTED
WATER
BEACH
CLOSED

A CAUSE FOR CONSERVATION

Conservation is the word for guarding the **environment**, including water, air, animals, and plants. We can't stop everyone from polluting. However, we can often do something when we find litter. We can throw it out. But sometimes cleaning up is too much for one person.

IN MANY PLACES, PEOPLE WHO ARE CAUGHT LITTERING MUST PAY A **FINE.**

TEAM EFFORT

One person might have a hard time cleaning up a whole beach, road, park, or neighborhood. A whole team or group would make the work go faster. Taking part in a cleanup is a way to be a conservation **champion**.

SOMETIMES A GROUP DOES CLEANUPS EVERY WEEK, EVERY MONTH, OR EVERY YEAR.

MAKING A PLAN

Successful cleanups follow steps. First, leaders decide on a date, time, and place for **volunteers** to meet. (Some places may need a local **official** to okay the cleanup.) Next, they spread the word through signs and **social media**. Then, they gather supplies such as trash bags and gloves. Finally, everyone gets to work!

A SIGN FOR A CLEANUP CAN BE HOMEMADE. REGULAR CLEANUPS MAY HAVE A SIGN LIKE THIS.

CLEAN FUN

Cleanups are a great way to meet other people who care about conservation. Ask an adult to find a cleanup you can do together. You'll learn more about cleanup efforts and how they work. And you'll learn that cleaning up can be fun when you do it with friends!

GRABBERS LIKE THIS ARE A GOOD WAY TO KEEP YOUR HANDS AWAY FROM DIRTY OR UNSAFE OBJECTS.

ACTIVITY

- Think of a place close to home you'd like to clean up.
- Ask an adult to help you organize a small cleanup effort.
- Ask friends to join you.
- Have supplies ready for them.
- Have fun working together!

SAFETY TIP!

Don't pick up sharp things, such as broken glass and sharp metal. Ask an adult for help with those.

GLOSSARY

champion: One who fights for a cause.

chemical: Matter that can be mixed with other matter to cause changes.

environment: The natural world in which a plant or animal lives.

fine: An amount of money paid as a punishment.

official: A person who has a position of responsibility in an organization.

pollution: The act of water or land becoming unsafe for people or animals.

social media: Websites and applications, also known as apps, used to create online communities.

volunteer: A person who works without being paid.

FOR MORE INFORMATION

BOOKS

Lewis, Cicely. *Imani at the Beach*. Minneapolis, MN: Lerner Publications, 2025.

Xie, Chelsea. *Volunteering for the Environment*. San Diego, CA: BrightPoint Press, 2022.

WEBSITES

Pollution
kids.nationalgeographic.com/science/article/pollution
Read more about pollution and the many problems it causes.

13 Ways to Save the Earth from Pollution
kids.nationalgeographic.com/nature/save-the-earth/article/13-ways-to-save-the-earth-from-pollution
Read more about cleanups and other ways to be a conservation champion!

INDEX